TO

FROM

DATE

INSPIRATIONAL *Peace*

AUSTRALIAN PHOTOGRAPHS BY KEN DUNCAN

PANOGRAPHS®
PUBLISHING PTY LTD

AMELIA EARHART

*Courage is the price that life
exacts for granting peace.*

Peace like a river - how refreshing that stream -
that calms deep within us, like a wonderful dream. PAM BONNER

FRONT COVER *Pastel Moorings, Shark Bay, WA*
PREVIOUS PAGE *Faithful Guardians, The Twelve Apostles, Vic*
THIS PAGE *Natural Arch, Gold Coast Hinterland, Qld*

Peace can be defined as the absence of conflict or hostility, yet there is nowhere we can go in this world where we will be completely free from conflict. Therefore, we need to be able to achieve and maintain inner peace, even when turmoil rages all around.

The beauty of nature has a very calming effect on the human spirit and the Australian photographs on the following pages have been specially chosen to bring you peace. I hope these images and the accompanying quotes soothe your soul, help you find sanctuary from the tensions of life and give you peace.

Ken Duncan

Peace I leave with you;

my peace I give you.

I do not give to you as the world gives.

Do not let your hearts be troubled

and do not be afraid.

Low Isles, Qld

*When the power of love overcomes
the love of power,
the world will know peace.*

THIS PAGE
Josephine Falls, Wooroonooran National Park, Qld

FOLLOWING PAGES
The Promise, Haasts Bluff, NT

KEN DUNCAN

Peace on earth starts with you and me.

Peace is liberty in tranquillity.

First Light, Terrigal, NSW

Peace is always beautiful.

THIS PAGE
Tulips, Wynyard, Tas

FOLLOWING PAGES
Stockman's Rest, Falls Creek, Vic

JOHN COUGAR MELLENCAMP

An honest man's pillow is his

peace of mind.

When you've seen beyond yourself,
then you may find,
peace of mind is waiting there.

Dividing Line, Kambalda, WA

GERALD JAMPOLSKY

Peace of mind comes from not wanting to change others.

THIS PAGE
Drifting Sands, Gunyah Beach, SA

FOLLOWING PAGES
Island Paradise, Hill Inlet, Qld

PSALM 85:10

Love and faithfulness meet together;

righteousness and peace kiss each other.

Imagine all the people living life in peace.
You may say I'm a dreamer,
but I'm not the only one.
I hope someday you'll join us, and the
world will be as one.

Weeping Willow, Yarra Valley, Vic

CARLOS SANTANA

The most valuable possession you can

own is an open heart.

The most powerful weapon you can be is

an instrument of peace.

THIS PAGE
Red Heart, Uluru, NT

FOLLOWING PAGES
Somersby Sanctuary, Somersby Falls, NSW

FRANCIS OF ASSISI

Lord, make me an instrument of thy peace.

Where there is hatred, let me sow love.

Peace is not absence of conflict,
it is the ability to handle conflict by
peaceful means.

Rising Force, Terrigal, NSW

If it is possible,
as far as it depends on you,
live at peace with everyone.

THIS PAGE
Sailor's Delight, Broome, WA

FOLLOWING PAGES
Misty Morning, Strzelecki Ranges, Vic

MOTHER TERESA

If we have no peace, it is because we have forgotten that we belong to each other.

*To be at peace with others you must be
at peace with yourself.*

Flinders Twilight, Flinders Ranges, SA

Peace is not merely a distant goal that we seek, but a means by which we arrive at that goal.

THIS PAGE
Red Road, Kata Tjuta, NT

FOLLOWING PAGES
Cape Leveque, WA

Peace is a daily, a weekly, a monthly process, gradually changing opinions, slowly eroding old barriers, quietly building new structures.

GEORGE A. SMITH

Man does find in Nature deliverance
from himself, oblivion of his past,
with peace and purity!

Snug Cove, Kangaroo Island, SA

42

The Lord bless you and keep you;
the Lord make His face shine on you
and be gracious to you;
the Lord turn his face toward you and
give you peace.

THIS PAGE
Dixons Kingdom Hut, Tas

FOLLOWING PAGES
Full Moon, Bungle Bungles, WA

KEN DUNCAN

Peace in our soul gives us confidence that

we are heading in the right direction.